Grandma's Pictures of the Past

By
Phil Cummings

Illustrated by
Loma Tilders

Tim and his dad were going to visit Grandma Kelly.

Up through the hills, and out of the city, they drove. Grandma Kelly lived in an old house in the country.

Tim loved going to visit his grandma. It was like an adventure.

Grandma Kelly's house was surrounded by trees and vines. Her yard was full of rusty old plows and broken-down tractors.

Tim loved to explore around his grandma's place. He always found things such as horseshoes, old bikes, and buried bottles.

When Tim and his father arrived at Grandma Kelly's house, her old dog, Rex, licked Tim's hands.

His grandma squeezed Tim hard. "Oh it's good to see you," she laughed. "Let me look at you." Tim stood tall.

"You know, Tim," said Grandma Kelly, "you look just like your father when he was a boy."

Tim liked Grandma Kelly's stories about his dad as a boy.

"He wore gray shorts with suspenders to school, Tim," said Grandma Kelly, as they walked inside. "And he was very good at marbles. He was always playing marbles."

"Were you, Dad?" asked Tim.

"Well, I didn't have computers and videos to keep me busy, remember," said Tim's father.

That night, a storm blew in.

As they sat by the fire, Tim told Grandma Kelly about his new computer game.

"It's great, Grandma," he said. "It's called Gremlin Gobble and you have to run away from the gremlins before they gobble you up."

Grandma Kelly laughed. "And to think we only had the radio when I was a girl, growing up in the country. We thought that was special—all those voices coming to us from far away."

Tim wondered about a world without television, videos, and computers.

"What did you and your friends do when you were a girl, Grandma?" he asked.

"Well," said Grandma Kelly, smiling, "we liked to skip, ride our bikes or our horses. We liked to explore. And we loved to watch the trains—the steam trains."

Grandma Kelly stood up from her chair and walked over to her cupboard by the old sewing machine. She took out a photo album and sat down again.

"Come and have a look at these," she said to Tim. "You'll see what the world was like when I was growing up."

Grandma Kelly's photo album was full of all sorts of things, not only photos, but postcards and newspaper clippings as well.

She turned to a photo of a family.

"This is my mom and dad," she said.
"And do you see that little girl?
 That's me!"

Grandma Kelly showed Tim everything in the album. He saw photos of…

old trains, old radios, old cars,

And there was a photo of his dad and his uncle when they were little, standing next to an old car.

"Which one is you, Dad?" Tim asked, looking at the photo.

"I'm the smaller one," Tim's father said, laughing.

Suddenly, there was a loud rumble of thunder and the lights went out.

"Oh no!" said Tim's father.

"I'm scared," said Tim.

"Don't worry," said Grandma Kelly. "I've got some old lamps here to light. I always keep them handy."

Suddenly, the room was filled with a soft yellow light as Grandma Kelly struck a match and lit one of her old lamps.

Tim thought it was exciting as he watched the big shadows on the walls. He looked around at all of his grandma's old things. "I really feel like I'm back in the old days now," he said.

"Ah yes," smiled Grandma Kelly. "Let's have some music, shall we?"

Grandma Kelly walked over to her piano and started playing. Tim and his father sang along to the songs they knew.

And you know, even though the songs were old ones, they knew quite a few of them.

The next morning, Tim woke to the sound of Grandma Kelly singing and whistling. Tim found her in the kitchen. The power was still off so she was using the old wood stove to make breakfast.

"Good morning, Grandma," said Tim.

"Good morning, Tim!" she sang, as steam puffed out of the kettle. "Now, this really is like the old days, isn't it?"

Tim sat in the warm kitchen eating his breakfast. He looked around at the old cupboards, tins, and photos. He watched the flames in the old stove flicker and dance. He watched his grandma wind up the old clock on the mantel and felt as though he had traveled back in a time machine.

After breakfast, Tim and his father had to go home.

Tim waved madly as they drove out of his grandma's winding, muddy driveway. He was going to tell his mom how he had traveled back in time at Grandma Kelly's house.

As they drove down through the hills, towards the city and home, Tim wondered what adventure he would have next time he visited Grandma Kelly.

When they got home, Tim thought about playing Gremlin Gobble on his computer but then decided to try something else.

"Hey Dad!" he called. "Let's play marbles."

And so...they did.